WOLVES POST

COLLECTION ONE

Twenty-two postcards
to benefit the
**INTERNATIONAL
WOLF CENTER**

Voyageur Press

Cover photograph copyright © by L. David Mech
Printed in Hong Kong
94   95   96   97   98   10   9   8   7   6

ISBN 0-89658-125-X

Distributed in Canada by Raincoast Books, 112 East Third Avenue, Vancouver, B.C. V5T 1C8

Published by Voyageur Press, Inc.
P.O. Box 338, 123 North Second Street, Stillwater, MN 55082 U.S.A.
612-430-2210, *fax* 612-430-2211

Please write or call, or stop by, for our free catalog of natural history publications. Our toll-free number to place an order or to obtain a free catalog is 800-888-WOLF (800-888-9653).

Educators, fundraisers, premium and gift buyers, publicists, and marketing managers: Looking for creative products and new sales ideas? Voyageur Press books are available at special discounts when purchased in quantities, and special editions can be created to your specifications. For details contact the marketing department.

The International Wolf Center

At the International Wolf Center, visitors experience the stirring howl of the wolf in the combined setting of museum and nature center. The center is located in Ely, Minnesota, in the heart of wolf range and the site of twenty-five years of wolf research. The center's mission of public education about the wolf and its interrelationships with other species is its driving force. There, visitors learn about the wolf's story, its habits, and its coexistence with other species and with humans. Contact the International Wolf Center for more information about membership, or join now at one of of the following levels and receive *International Wolf*, the quarterly educational magazine for IWC members.

- ☐ $25   Lone Wolf
- ☐ $50   Wolf Pack
- ☐ $100 Wolf Associate
- ☐ $500 Wolf Sponsor
- ☐ $1000 Alpha Wolf

International Wolf Center
1396 Highway 169
Ely, Minnesota 55731-8129 U.S.A.
1-800-ELY-WOLF (1-800-359-9653)

A four-week-old wolf pup.

The wolf is a magnificent wild animal, shy and secretive, poised and alert. In a sense, the wolf is familiar to everyone because it is the forerunner of the dog. Nevertheless, few people have had the privilege of seeing a wolf in its natural surroundings.

Originally, wolves ranged over all the northern hemisphere. Now they are gone from much of North America and western Europe. Minnesota, Canada, Alaska, and the Soviet Union have some of the largest wolf populations. But wolves are considered threatened in Minnesota, and they are endangered elsewhere in the forty-eight contiguous states.

Wolves live in family packs that are made up of a set of parents, a litter of pups, and a few remaining yearlings and older offspring. They feed mainly on deer, moose, caribou, elk, bison, musk oxen, and other large animals.

The International Wolf Center's *Wolves Postcard Collection* features glimpses of wolves in many settings, taken by some of the world's foremost wolf photographers.

The photographers for this collection of postcards are Durward L. Allen of Purdue University, West Lafayette, Indiana; Fred H. Harrington of Mount St. Vincent University, Halifax, Nova Scotia; Karen Hollett of Mount St. Vincent University, Halifax, Nova Scotia; Layne Kennedy of Minneapolis, Minnesota; L. David Mech, Vice Chairman of the International Wolf Center, Ely, Minnesota; Robert Ream of University of Montana, Missoula, Montana; Thomas J. Meier of Denali National Park, Denali, Alaska; Rolf O. Peterson of Michigan Technological University, Houghton, Michigan; and Lynn L. Rogers of Ely, Minnesota.

These photographers have generously donated their artwork for the *Wolves Postcard Collection,* so that all royalties earned from the sale of the postcards can be donated to the International Wolf Center in Ely, Minnesota.

The start of a stalk.

Wolves travel tirelessly.

Generally, wolves travel in packs.

Wolf pups are born in dens.

From the *Wolves Postcard Collection.* Copyright © 1990 by
L. David Mech. Voyageur Press, 123 N. 2nd St., Stillwater, MN 55082

The wolf is at home in the north.

Adult wolves regurgitate food to pups.

From the *Wolves Postcard Collection.* Copyright © 1990 by
L. David Mech. Voyageur Press, 123 N. 2nd St., Stillwater, MN 55082

A lone wolf out to seek its fortune.

From the *Wolves Postcard Collection.* Copyright © 1990 by
Thomas J. Meier. Voyageur Press, 123 N. 2nd St., Stillwater, MN
55082

Wolves are ever alert.

Wolf pups need shelter.

The color of wolves varies from black to white, with shades in between.

A pup greets an adult.

A four-month-old wolf pup.

A tired arctic wolf.

Wolves are affectionate.

Wolves must feed on other animals.

A moose-eye's view of a wolf.

Even wolves must sleep.

Arctic wolves are white.

A lone arctic wolf washing up in the river after a musk-oxen kill.

A wolf pack is a family.